CAUTION

Keep in mind that this is a lifetime investment. Do not rely on information from friends.

Choose the tattoo artist that is right for you. The artist should have the training and license to provide you with a clean safe service, and provide you with proper care for the tattoo.

WELCOME

Here you will find hundreds of tribal tattoos ready to be traced, colored or inked.

We hope you find this book something you really enjoy.

Thanks!!

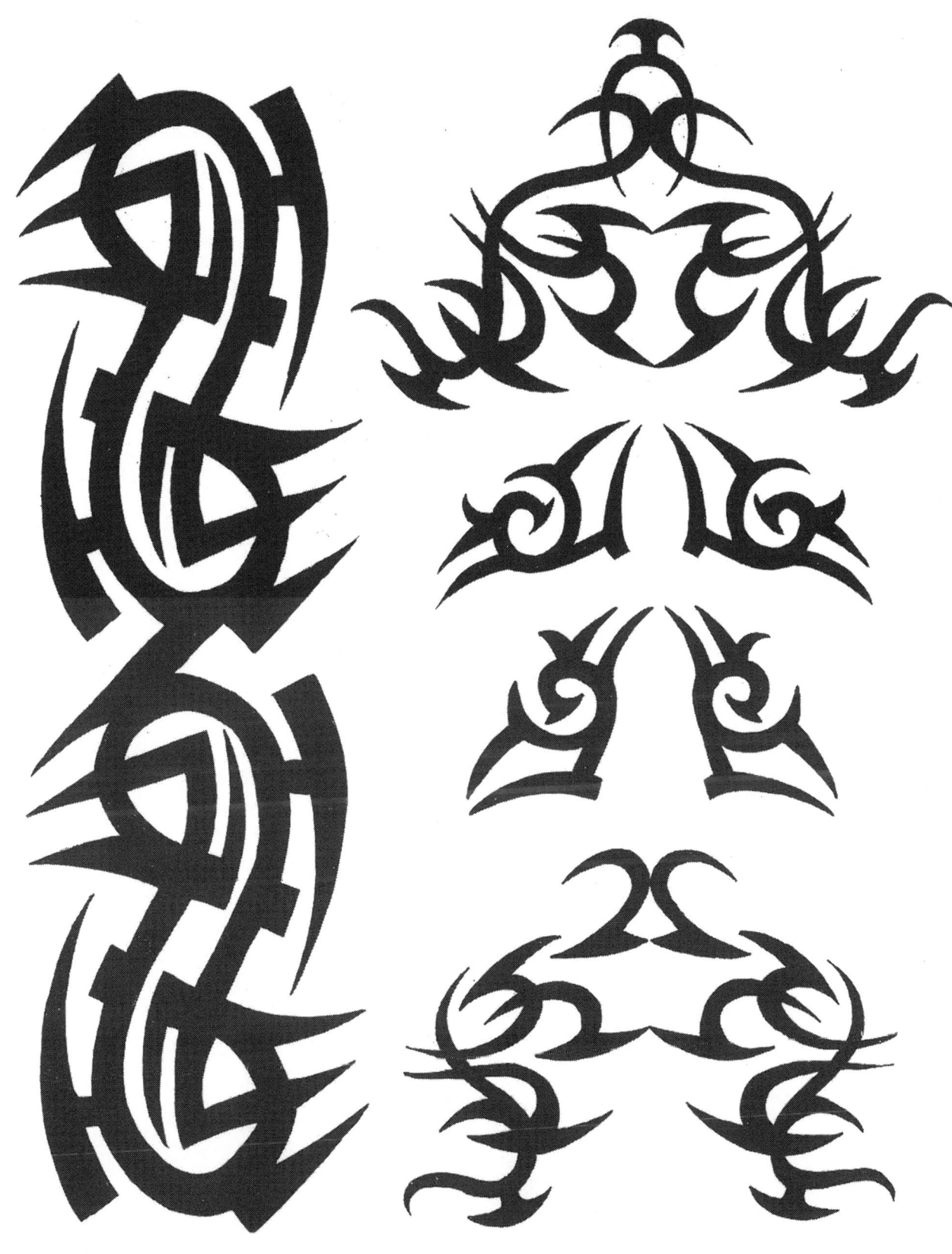

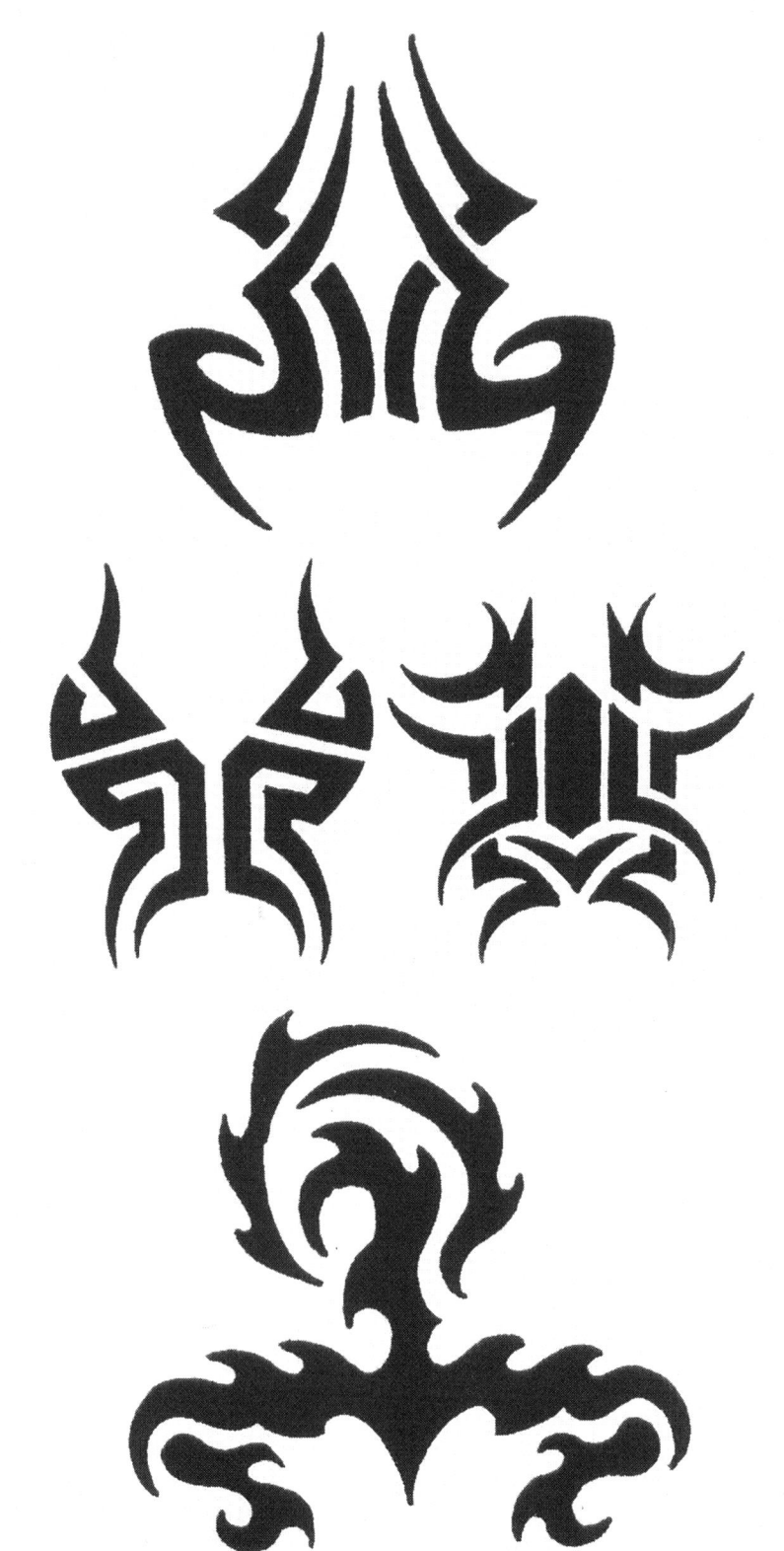

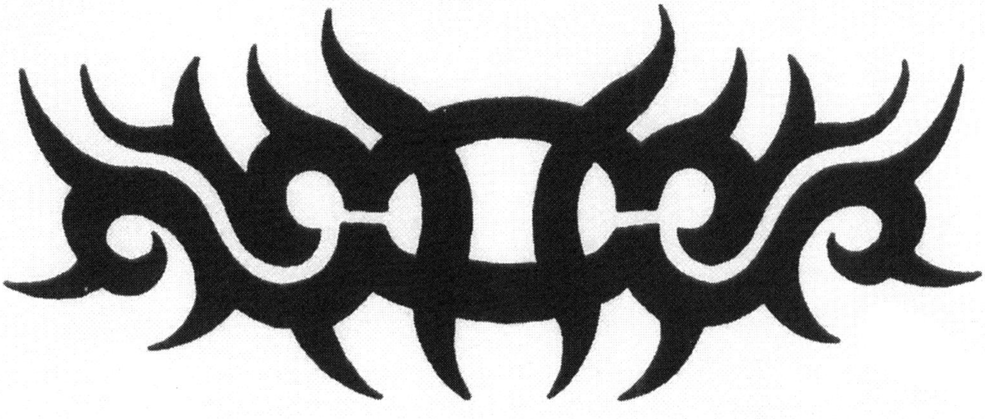

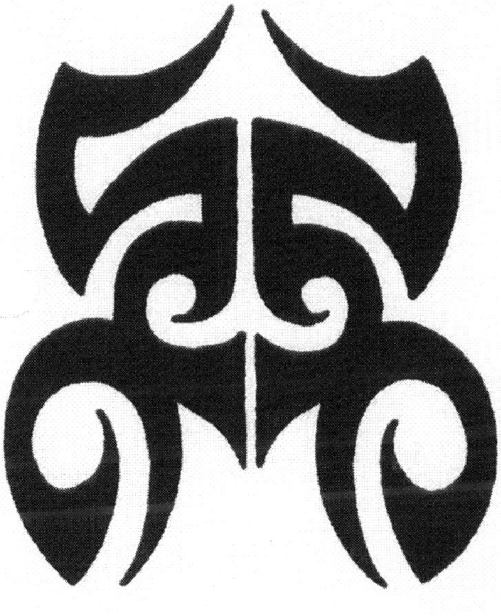

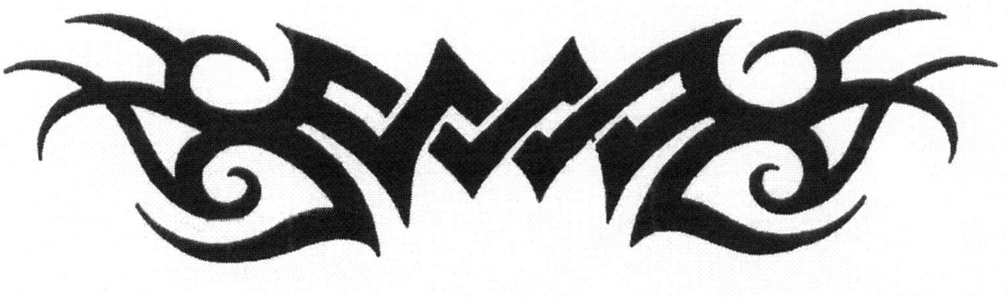

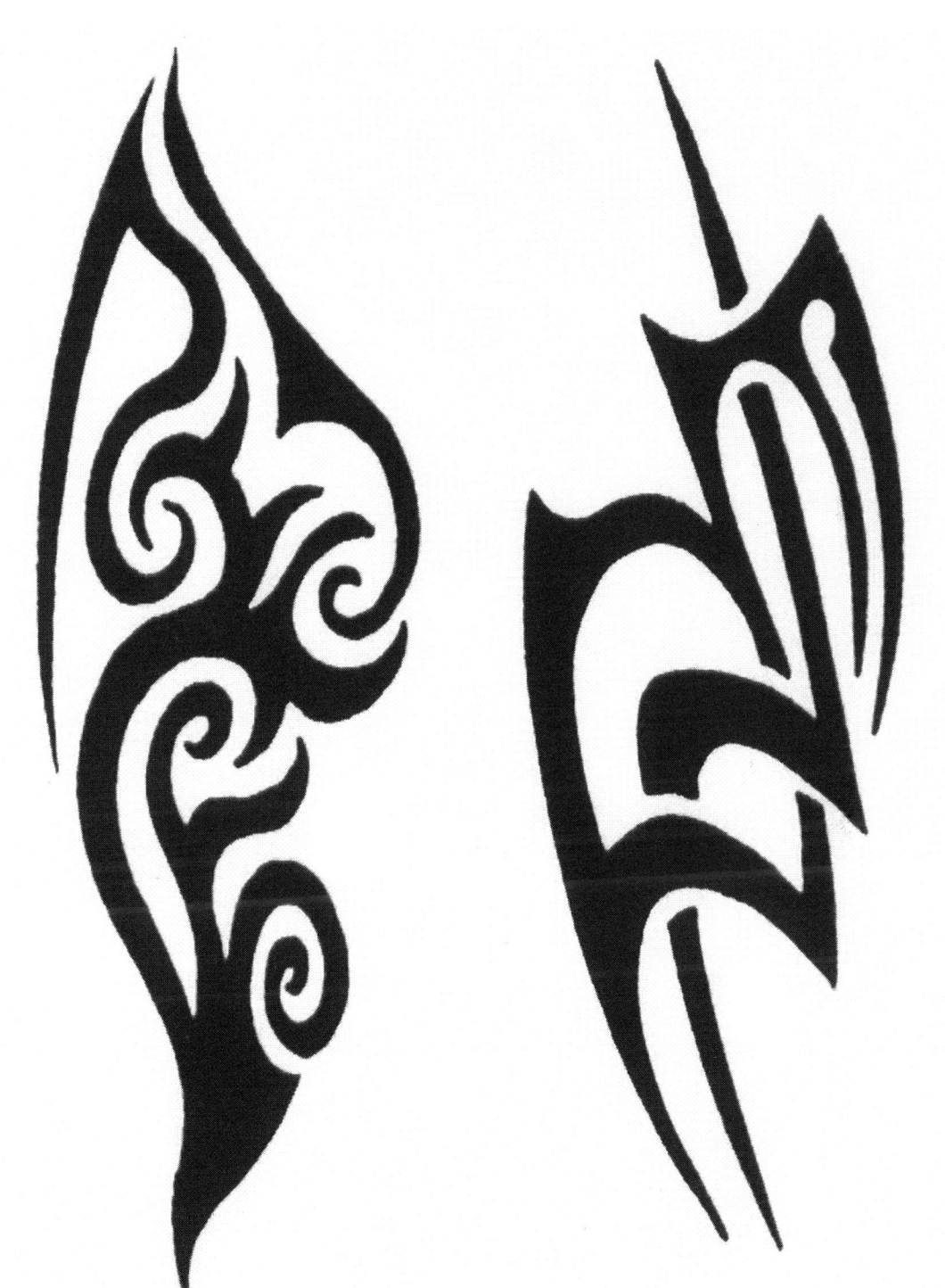

29100265R00066

Printed in Great Britain
by Amazon